BODY POLITIC

BODY POLITIC

TONY FLYNN

BLOODAXE BOOKS

ISBN: 1 85224 129 2

First published 1992 by
Bloodaxe Books Ltd,
P.O. Box 1SN,
Newcastle upon Tyne NE99 1SN.

Bloodaxe Books Ltd acknowledges
the financial assistance of Northern Arts.

Cover reproduction by V & H Reprographics, Newcastle upon Tyne.

Cover printing by J. Thomson Colour Printers Ltd, Glasgow.

Printed in Great Britain by
Billing & Sons Limited, Worcester.

In memory of my father
DANIEL FRANCIS FLYNN
1914-1989

Acknowledgements

Acknowledgements are due to the editors of the following publications in which some of these poems first appeared: *Encounter, The Honest Ulsterman, The Literary Review, London Magazine* and *Quarto*. Fourteen of the poems were published in *A Rumoured City*, edited by Douglas Dunn (Bloodaxe Books, 1982).

Tony Flynn wishes to thank the Arts Council of Great Britain for their award of a writer's bursary.

Contents

*If way to the Better there be, it exacts
a full look at the Worst.*

HARDY

The Bride
(for Piotr M.)

They made their way,
his family and her family,
towards the grave –

Past the lamp-post
they strung him from
once he was dead,

and the shipyard that
troops now patrol
night and day

where workers shuffle
behind the gates
like lifers who trudge

the exercise yard.
At Easter she was
to have married the boy.

All down the street
each frozen patch
of blood under ice

looked like a map
of their little country.
By the graveside she let

her wedding-dress fall
like a long night of snow
on the coffin lid.

Later, alone
in her narrow bed, she wept
her wedding vows to the wall.

No comfort came –
only this, at last –
her body a ridge

of gentle peaks,
her groom
a slow cloud descending.

Domestic Interior

(i.m. Marianella García Villas)

Three days ago
they found another tortured corpse,
as yet to be identified.

Somehow the family already knows.

She whispers to him
her sister's last letter to both of them –

...I am struggling
for life, a real and dignified
life – I do not want
to die...

Bugged walls record
the evidence against them now;

for this they could be disappeared.

Through a long
sleepless night they've watched the moon
foreshadow what's to come of them –

her crumpled white dress
like a shroud on the chair.

Come, hold me close –
and breathe in the candlesmoke, cat-piss, and rain;
lay my head on your belly
and pull up the sheet...
                              Tomorrow
they must come for us.

They pray and curse
God and their prayers –

                    ...should ever

our bodies be found
again, bury us

together where
a small, fresh stream
for so long dammed

might burst its banks and wash away
the smell of blood that clots the air
we once breathed easily and free.

And wash away
their semen from her
severed trunk.

The Servant's Tale

I rise, and am invisible
about the place...From the moment
I first kneel

at the cold hearth
with wood to set the fire there,
I am his servile

ghost of the rooms.
My name he neither knew
nor knows – But once he came late

to my attic room, stumbled
drunk to my narrow bed...And I
complied – Not a word of command

from him but I lay
obedient beneath him there.
So easily did I attend,

I might have been pouring
his favourite wine. On his leaving I smoothed
the crumpled sheets

as if I were
clearing his place after dinner –
Day after day

and all through the house,
my snowfield, my linen field,
trampled and fouled.

Elegy

(i.m. Primo Levi)

1

They numbered you,
and they numbered your bones –
Häftling 174517,
Block 3.

2

No pillar of fire
but a corpse-candle burned
wherever you looked
after what you had seen –

And mass graves
the watchtowers' search-
lights lit still
cast their shadows

to rot in the world
in the shape of your shadow
wherever it
falls.

3

A year now since
your suicide,
though they buried you
alive over half a lifetime ago.

Autumnal

Soon you will learn,
very soon you will learn

that the language
you have grown up with,

the language you have lived with
like your own family

for so many years
deserts you here – Words

turn traitor and betray
their own meanings.

So that when they tell you
how the woman and children

who were herded from the train
along with you

but whom you have not
seen since

were given showers
and put to work elsewhere,

you will know
what did not happen.

Just as you will know
that the thin, continuous pillars

of black smoke rising
night and day

behind huts
at the edge of the camp

are not from bonfires
burning dead leaves.

The Interview

When she asked him, in the blinding
glare of the studio-lights, how it had been that winter
with the emaciated dead and the half-dead piled
in heaps outside the wooden huts, he

scrounged his reply
from the rubble of language they'd left him with –

(as if for the first time he were piecing together
the shards of his own shattered reflection)

'I remember snow –
All night it snowed.
                    And in the morning
                                        the ground
no longer moved...'

Veterans

We planned in cellars
at the burnt-out
heart of our city –

Conspirators, the threatened
who fought from sewers
and bombed factories;

from a gutted church
where sudden flares
blazed through a crucified

stained-glass
Christ, and
shattered saints

scarred our knees
as we crawled to shadow
like rats –

(our teeth
at every booted
heel.) Now

we are
free, and our teeth
rot. The enemy

has gone to ground,
and seeps like
gas through

curtained rooms –
under pillows
at midnight –

from the open
mouths
of our sleeping wives.

Body Politic

'Both are true, and both are to be preserved in contradiction'
RUSSELL JACOBY

The bag of bones
shivering under a blanket

of excrement is not
a poet hungering out

what's left of her
conviction, or

something to do
with the workings of the state.

Our Lady of Guadalupe

I

His bedroom window opened on
the church across from his cheap hotel
so that his wardrobe-mirror might
reflect the black Madonna there. Mornings
he would wake to her, would
lie and look at her before he knelt
and pressed himself against the glass, as if
to take her in his arms

and like a bride-
groom carry her over
the threshold...Or
like the man
who would have her against
her will (doggy
fashion for a wager
with His Eminence, the Cardinal).

II

The massed white
congregation cheers
the city fathers who
decree that she be
burned in the square for her secret
communion with women in those parts.
She-devil! Hag! His Eminence
caws, *Black*

beldame begone! And
smiles sly
smiles, and winks at his
familiars all the while – Hissed
whisperings blister and spit
on his lips, *Burn*
all the God-forsaken whores –

(*That or they boil our balls for broth.*)

Burnings

Dug up black
dismembered doll (headless

torso, legs
splayed, ruined.)

– Burned her with the rest
of the rubbish.

      * * *

Little Kaysha stares
(transfixed)

into the flames,
clings

tight to her
grandmother's sari.

      * * *

The old woman recalls
her wedding-

sari's blaze of
reds and golds (how

fiercely consumed she was
in its folds.)

      * * *

Kaysha (trans-
fixed) sees

clearly through the
smoky haze:

White fire –
Black sister.

Lying Low

I am keeping notebooks, journals, in a perfect longhand, a scrupulous calligraphy, copperplate on vellum.

Rapid, on-the-spot jottings precede the final painstaking entries. No corrections or erasions mar my cursive script – mistakes dictate that I begin again.

Today I have numbered the bones of a small, dead bird; plucked and counted every feather; I have identified each particle of food that remained in its crop after death.

And when the sky flames above the capital, my night is speaking names in the dark, christening specimens pressed under glass, *Carex montana...vulpina...nigra...*

Keeping my head down, lying low.

En Famille

With my head shaved and my face
painted blue, my nipples pierced and ear-rings

through, I'm ready to start the show.
The curtain rises. Birdsong and the blinding light.

Downstairs, in the wings,
my two small sons and their father rehearse

our dénouement, their sub-plot,
my fall.

Lullaby
(for Katie & Ellen)

You will remember
none of this – these hours

in my arms, cradling
your fevered head against

my shirt – your small skull's
watermark impressed above my heart –

this room, the lullaby I sing
to your troubled dreams.

Since You Left

It is late and the house
is quiet...Late, and I am alone
in the room where I worked.

Behind the curtain are windows
like row upon row of open graves;
and there are dead stars there that shine
more brightly than the risen moon.

Your young face framed
by a cold white sky
smiles down from the wall
above my desk –
               You are aboard
ship, ready to sail, and the decks are packed

with waving strangers who've watched me grow old.

Boats for Hire

Drifting through fallen
floating leaves, trailing its oars

like two broken wings, our rowing boat
nudged the muddy bank, startling a swan and his mate.

We watched them rise,
followed their climb away from us,

and wished for them
a quiet lake, where only

their own reflections glide
between them on the water.

And you cannot pay
to row across it.

Light-Years
(for Sally)

Struggling home,
weighed down by the satchel
they'd harnessed me to, I'd
stumble knee-deep

through snow-drifts
on dark afternoons
after school (gazing
up at a wintry sky) and

day-dreaming stretch on
tiptoe to touch
cold stars that burned
above our house...

And so it is
with you and me –
There are light-years
between us.

Between the Lines
(for Patrick & Sarah)

She's hassling her brother yet again
who's struggling with *Lear* for his last exam –

'...A year or maybe more ago
and we were a thousand miles away...

Remember the cove we found that night
lost on our way to somewhere else? –

Hard to believe we were ever there...'

In no time she has him adrift with her –

And the soft
roar of distant cars

is the sea,

swelling and lifting our land-locked hearts.

Gleanings

As if my soul
were a scattered threshing
of this and that, which
now your sure hands compose –

A gathering up
of lost threads, random
gleanings woven into this
seamless gift –

          Our true selves
at last,
we share a strange
gratuitous delight –

our marriage-bed, and wedding night.

Piano-Hands

You told me once
how, as a girl, you'd often
cried yourself to sleep

because you didn't have
piano-hands. Slender
hands sleek

in expensive gloves, or
hesitant like
birds above a sunlit

vase, recall
those nights, your tears,
and my deceit –

I swore I loathed
such elegance, scorned
manicured coquettes, all the while

dreaming of frenzied
red nails, long
fingers to tangle my hair.

The Fish

Late afternoon
in your attic flat,
on a mattress that cushioned
the bare floorboards, you

seemed at ease, and
talked about the fish you'd watched
that day in the stream behind
the old mill –
                How it
dozed by the bank
for hours, so still
it might have been dead –

'But so
perfectly still, against
the flow, it had
to be alive,' you said.

Then you fell asleep
for the first time in months
without booze or the usual
pills, and hardly
moved until I felt
you edge from my arms
in tears.
                Dreaming,
did you
dip your hand
to touch a stillness
under water, and
touching water
                dart
a fish?

Portugal

Sal, meaning
literally

salt –
(colloquially

'essence of woman').
Sal, still

salting my tongue
after all these years.

Seasons

I

Out of sight of all eyes but mine
she's crouched in tangled undergrowth –

Her full summer skirt hitched up
round her waist, she

seems to float on its crimson cloud,
scattering yellow stars at her feet.

II

Blood-red moons
that burn in her eyes, ferine

and venereal through
the liquorice fringe of her beaded hair.

Watch as she steps
                from the dark doorway –
how her undressing might melt fresh-fallen snow.

The Dandy's Dream

'...to live and die before a mirror...'
BAUDELAIRE

How I love all
these mirrors, this glass!
To die like this would be

perfection – The blade held
to my throat, wide eyes
following its slow

descent (careful not to
graze or scar) and then the
breathless

pause
above my cock – dreaming
its soft fall

against my thigh.
Perfection: to fix
the grimace in my dying eyes,

and then to leave
this room, my body,
and the glass voyeur.

Les Poètes Maudits

After cutting a dashing figure
in the capital, seducing women
from every level of society –
rumours even of a Royal conquest –
I shall ruin myself at cards,
drink my health to its ebb,
retire to the country – a small
run-down estate – and die,
leaving my beautiful daughter penniless,

at the mercy of a writer who
invents a chance affair, sudden
marriage to a banker's son; children;
all that she desires; and for me
a grave she'll visit every spring
with violets: forgiven, remembered only
for presents on birthdays,
surprises at Christmas, what I
might have been but for the world.

Saint Francis
(for Sally)

Crumbs of soil smudge
fingertips that lift
the small egg from its nest.

Cupped in his calloused
palm and held
perfectly still

to his ear,
he listens
and can hear,

through grey–green
speckled shell,
the dreaming white.

Father Michael's Waking Dream

She calls to him now
from the edge of the pool —

Bless me,
Father, for I have
sinned...

Laughing, she
steps from her thin
blue dress —

                    ...sticky
red leaves
in your matted hair, O
my sweet, my
precious one...

and turns from the trees
towards him.
                    His vision
swims and blurs.

He blinks —

The black dog sprawled
across her shadow, nosing her grassy
cleft, might be his cassock
sloughed on the lawn,

or his own shadow
darker on hers.

Dubrovlag

('The Oak Leaf Camps')

I

Your shaved head hung
                    like a frozen moon
in the starless vault of your freezing cell,

where you knelt

in big old boots
                    & calico dress
and whispered your prayers to the wall.

II

'Interminable days...

And my mortal soul inches
the walls of its cell
                    (shrinks

into itself)
            dissolves
like a salt-sprinkled
slug to no more
                    than a stain...'

III

Only when they had stripped you
of everything

did you redeem it all – and more –

(How secret a seamstress you were,
embroidering poem after poem
on the flawless fabric of your heart
& storing them there –
                    Your hidden
testament & tapestry of pain.)

IV

In no time
        the broken stove
was your ikon,

& bending on one knee
to fix it
        a genuflection.

Bread & water –

and the black crust was your eucharist.

The Wedding

Her father's shadow
slobbers behind her,

and yet he smiles
as if nothing

had ever happened.
And no one sees

her silent
immolation there –

how in that instant
at the altar

her white veil chars
to a spray of ash – Which

blows through her eyes
and stings them to tears.

Christina's Birthday

Crumpled pants caught
round one leg – a froth of cream
on the grass at your feet –
where you squat out of sight

in the wet underbush,
and laugh up at me,
half-surprised by the sudden
soft splattering hiss.

Watching you brings back
another day, and I am
eight-years old again –
Christina blows her candles out...

And then the game
is hide-and-seek – Theresa
whispers in my ear, *I'll sit on you –
they'll never guess!* She smiles;

I kneel, and help her lift
her summer dress above my head –
breathing the blood-red, pungent cloud –
then crouch, and let her cover me...

You call and
wave, scrambling from
your sulphurous nest of rotting
fern – skirt still hitched

up round your waist –
a purple leaf
sealed to your thigh, just like
Theresa's birthmark there –

the very same
she teased would taste
like wine, should I
dare gently bite and lick.

The Butcher

As if she were coring
an apple, she'd
twisted the knife
in her six-month-old

daughter's vagina.
God the Father,
she said,
had visited her

in the form
of an ordinary man –
Looming above her, his
bloodied apron slapped

her face, flapped
in her eyes
like a big, black wing
that blotted out the sun.

The voice that thundered
in her head
splintered her mind,
as the cleaver splits

the chopping-block.
His lowly hand-
maid, she performed
his every command to the letter.

Walls

She died in 1953.
Night and day for twenty years,

time and again, religiously,
he's wandered these dark, Victorian wards,

running his fingers along the walls,
tracing her name in intricate whorls, as if

to divine her gentle voice
in cracks the flowered paper hides.

Storms

1

My mother's gypsy faith
was on its knees
whenever thunder roared –
Lightning floored her,
had her scrambling on all fours
under the big oak
kitchen table,
dragging us along with her –
where she shook for what seemed
like hours on end,
until the sky
brightened briefly again.

2

The charge nurse risks
a joke as the doctor leaves
the ward –

'Drugged up to
the eyeballs and
still

depressed?...Time,
me thinks,
for the live-wire waltz...'

(– And I'm back there
with her, cowed
on that cold, linoleum floor.)

3

Old foetal thumb-
suckers crouched
                    in the dark,
desperate
that the table hold.

Recovery

After months on
the ward there is only

this – one
day at a time –

(...the way
shell-shocked young

veterans must
scrounge their own shadows

in futile hope of
even a glimpse

of how it all once made
some sort of sense...)

The Black Guitar

Come, follow me,
hissed the wily noose,

garland your neck
with my roses and fern –

Come, let me tighten
the knot at your throat...

For my rope winds down
to the small cemetery

where every headstone
bears your name

and two dates chiselled
under moss

which we
alone, my love, can see.

I.Q.

At his junior school, they called him
jungle bunny, sambo, and once, *nigger.*
He became more and more 'withdrawn' –
His teacher wrote in one report

that he experienced great difficulty in relating
to children of his own age, both in the classroom
setting and socially. (She did not write
that because he was lonely, because he was angry,

and because he wanted to be
like them, he took a pumicestone, nail brush,
and some DAZ, and scraped and scrubbed
at his black face

until it bled.) The school nurse dressed
his superficial wounds, but one deep cut
required stitches. They sent him home...
A letter followed, *Dear Mrs C —,* in which the Head

informed her he'd referred
her son to the school's psychologist –
Who saw him, eventually, twice,
and administered various I.Q. tests.

She found him uncooperative,
and noted this. He was assessed
as well below average, and certainly within
the lower range of ability.

She was confident that
he would never survive
in a mainstream school – '...his quite acute
remedial needs demand

dramatic intervention soon...' A small
and structured teaching base where he'd receive
the close support of well-trained staff
was deemed appropriate at this stage.

Ten years later, he left
his residential school for maladjusted boys
with, '...no
formal qualifications...

Sullen, resentful
of authority,
and with a chip on his shoulder
which can only lead to further, more serious trouble...'

Also, under MEDICAL,
'...Distinguishing marks: small
scar above left eye – result
of self-inflicted injury in early years...'

Preferred Terms

(His head –

like something from
the offal bowl,

fashioned in the butcher's
bloody hands.)

Down's Syndrome please,
the young consultant interjects.

But she will have nothing to do
with their preferred terms –

Mongol, she says, *is what he is.*

(And gags
on her own words –

like gristle
she chews over
and over

but can't swallow –

And swallows.)

Punks

From a distance, and
momentarily, their orange heads

blaze and swirl
like sea-flowers straggled

by wild currents.
Closer, and you will see

a glue-bag hangs from every mouth
like the ghost

of a wasted lung.
Get too close

and it's like watching
speeded-up film

of a rose hit
by blight – how it

rots on the stem in
seconds.

Suburban Couple Leave a Spanish Hotel

At odds with trivia –
how much of bliss depends on
who, without contention,
feeds the cat.

Their visit magnifies regret.

Imagine them home,
confronting a desolate doorstep –

Watch them write
and then put out a note,

Dear Milkman,
                    We are back,
and need milk

desperately...

Oracle

The old Greek
fisherman lounged

in his boat
(crumpled and charred

like a brown paper bag
blown from the fire

that burned on the beach)
and crackled his jokes

at our expense,
'So white my friends –

Like bottles of milk!...'
Did we embrace,

embody, or fulfil
a prophecy later

that night
when I drank her down

in the thirsty dark,
and she lapped the cream off of me?

Cinematic

A white linen sheet draped over what was
her grandmother's treasured chest of drawers,
and candles loll
their yellow tongues against the dark.

She kneels at her makeshift altar and prays
that what feels like a film of a stranger's life
be shot again with a different end,
screened with the last scene cut from the reel.

But the small
shadow inches its grey ghost across
a slow-motion rush of December days –
By spring it will eclipse them all.

Thaw

From her bedroom
window we watched the snow

blossom bare trees against the pane –
a last spring proffered out of time...

(I weather alone the long
slow thaw,

and pray this
weighted branch might

lift, weeping
her brief season's end as it stirs.)

Last Rites

In nomine Patris, et Filii...

His hands flutter in the air above her –
candlelight trembles weak birds on the wall.

Her bony fingers clasp
a silver crucifix against
her breast.

          When her thin
tongue flicks
across her lips, he thinks how like
a lizard she looks
pinned by some cruel child to this cold sheet.

In the next room,
the old woman's son is on his knees

pleading with her favourite dress.

Blackbird
(for my father)

By the time he died,
he'd wasted away so badly that
his four sons only had the weight
of his soul to carry shoulder-high –

Lighter even than
blown eggs are – (still
cushioned on straw and cotton wool
in a battered old shoe-box under the bed).

Over the last few
lonely months, his wife has nursed
the prized box in her lap most days –
And cups a freckled

shell in her palm,
pressing it gently to
her lips, as though she might breathe
the living yolk back into it.